Great Songs of the 20th Century
1900-1950

Wise Publications
London/New York/Paris/Sydney/Copenhagen/Madrid

WIN

Music compiled by Peter Evans and Peter Lavender
Song background notes by Michael Kennedy
Cover and book design by Studio Twenty, London
Cover photographs courtesy Corbis & Hulton Getty

Exclusive Distributors:
Music Sales Limited
8-9 Frith Street,
London W1V 5TZ, England.
Music Sales Pty Limited
120 Rothschild Avenue,
Rosebery, NSW 2018,
Australia.

Order No. AM959189
ISBN 0-7119-7418-7

Your Guarantee of Quality
As publishers, we strive to produce every book to the highest
commercial standards. This book has been carefully designed to
minimise awkward page turns and to make playing from it a real pleasure.
Particular care has been given to specifying acid-free, neutral-sized paper
made from pulps which have not been elemental chlorine bleached.
This pulp is from farmed sustainable forests and was produced with
special regard for the environment. Throughout, the printing and
binding have been planned to ensure a sturdy, attractive publication
which should give years of enjoyment.
If your copy fails to meet our high standards, please inform
us and we will gladly replace it.

Music Sales' complete catalogue describes thousands of titles and is
available in full colour sections by subject, direct from Music Sales.
Please state your areas of interest and send a cheque/postal order
for £1.50 for postage to:
Music Sales Limited, Newmarket Road,
Bury St. Edmunds, Suffolk IP33 3YB.

www.internetmusicshop.com

Daddy Wouldn't Buy Me A Bow Wow

Words & Music by Joseph Tabrar

Joseph Tabrar's catchy ditty was an immediate hit on the music halls from 1893 onwards for Leeds born Vesta Victoria. The composer was born in London in 1857 and wrote for many stars, including Marie Lloyd and George Leybourne, before his death in 1931.

love my lit- tle cat, I do, its coat is oh so warm, it

comes each day with me to school, and sits up - on the form. When

teach - er says, "Why do you bring that lit - tle pet of yours?" I

tell her that my bring my cat a - long with me be - cause—

Dad - dy would - n't buy me a bow - wow (bow - wow), Dad - dy would - n't buy me a

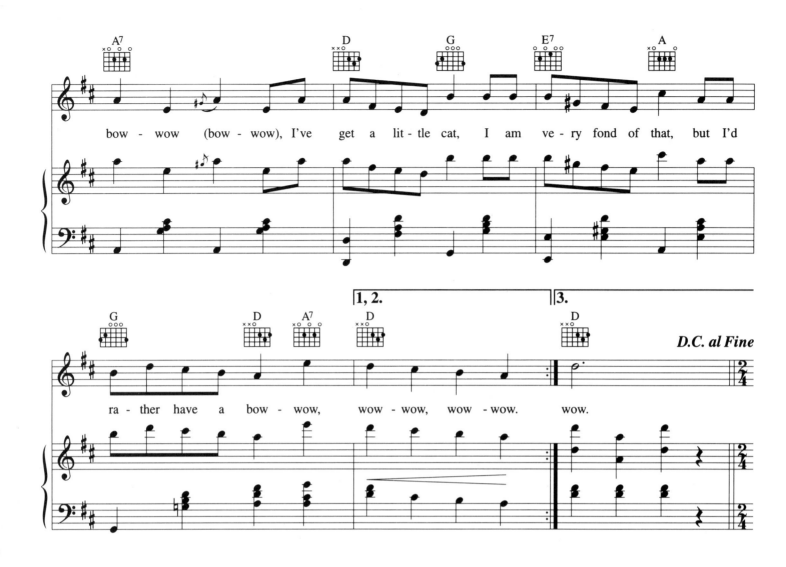

Verse 2:
We used to have two tiny dogs
Such pretty little dears
But Daddy sold 'em 'cos they used
To bite each other's ears
I cried all day – at eight at night
Papa sent me to bed
When ma came home and wip'd my eyes
I cried again and said –

Verse 3:
I'll be so glad when I get old
To do just as I please
I'll have a dozen bow-wows then
A parrot, and some bees
Whene'er I see a tiny pet
I'll kiss the little thing
'Twill remind me of the time gone by
When I would cry, and sing –

Daisy Bell

Words & Music by Harry Dacre

London born (1860) Harry Dacre emigrated to America where his greatest success 'Daisy Bell' (A Bicycle Built For Two) was introduced by vaudeville star Katie Lawrence in 1892. She brought the song to London and repeated her success on the music halls. Dacre returned to London, where he died, in 1922.

1. There is a flow-er with-in my heart,
(Verses 2 & 3 see block lyric)

Dai - - - sy, Dai - - - sy!

Plant - ed one day by a glanc - ing dart,

plant - ed by Dai - sy Bell!

Whe - ther she loves me or loves me not,

some - times it's hard to tell;

I'm half cra - - - - zy, all for the love of you! It won't be a styl - - - ish mar - riage, I can't af - ford a car - riage, but

Verse 2:
We will go "tandem" as man and wife
Daisy, Daisy!
"Ped'ling" away down the road of life
I and my Daisy Bell!

When the road's dark we can both despise
P'licemen and "lamps" as well
There are "bright lights" in the dazzling eyes
Of beautiful Daisy Bell!

Verse 3:
I will stand by you in "wheel" or woe
Daisy, Daisy!
You'll be the bell(e) which I'll ring, you know!
Sweet little Daisy Bell!

You'll take the "lead" in each "trip" we take,
Then if I don't do well
I will permit you to use the brake
My beautiful Daisy Bell!

Another smash success for Harry Dacre, 'I'll Be Your Sweetheart' (1899) was a favourite of music hall star Marie Kendall, an older relative of Kay Kendall, of Genevieve fame. The song was used as the title tune for a 40s film about music publishing piracy that starred Peter Graves and Margaret Lockwood.

I'll Be Your Sweetheart

Words & Music by Harry Dacre

1. One day I saw two lov-ers in a
(Verses 2 & 3 see block lyric)
gar - den, a lit - tle lad and lass with gold - en hair. They

looked as sweet as hon-ey in a bee - hive and so I stood and watched the youth-ful

pair, the lad all blush-ing gave the maid a kiss, then

ten - der - ly he whis - pered this.

I'll be your sweet - heart

Verse 2:
The blue bells were accepted by the maiden
She said "I'll keep them safely all my life
But then suppose you meet some other lady
And I should never be your darling wife
He shook his head and took another kiss
Then once again he whispered this:

Verse 3:
The years flew by and once again I saw them
They stood before the alter hand in hand
A handsome pair I never shall forget them
The happiest young couple in the land
And once again he took the loving kiss
Then passionately whispered this:

I Do Like To Be Beside The Seaside

Words & Music by John A. Glover-Kind

Blackpool Tower's famous organist Reginald Dixon adopted the jolly 'I Do Like To Be Beside The Seaside', by the Edwardian composer John A. Glover-Kind, as his signature tune. It was featured in the film The Adventures Of Sherlock Holmes and was a favourite for music hall legend Florrie Forde.

Con spirito

1. Ev-er-y-one de-lights to spend their sum-mer's ho-li-
(*Verses 2 & 3 see block lyric*)

day,_____ down be-side the side of the sil-ver-y

quite a no - ve - ty,_____ I save up all the mo - ney I can while

win - ter's grim and grey,_____ then off I run to

have some fun where the bal - my bree - zes play. Oh! I

do like to be be - side the sea - side,_____ I

Verse 2:

Timothy went to Blackpool for the day last Eastertide
To see what he could see by the side of the sea
Soon as he reached the station there the first thing he espied
Was the wine lodge door stood open invitingly
To quench his thirst he toddled inside and called out for a 'wine'
Which grew to eight or nine 'til his nose began to shine
Said he "What people see in the sea I'm sure I fail to see"
So he caught the train back home again, then to his wife said he:

Verse 3:

William Sykes the burglar he'd been out to work one night
Filled his bag with jewels, cash and plate
Constable Brown felt quite surprised when William hove in sight
Said he "The hours you're keeping are far too late"
So he grabbed him by the collar and lodged him safe and sound in jail
Next morning looking pale Bill told a tearful tale
The Judge said "For a couple of months, I'm sending you away."
Said Bill "How kind! Well if you don't mind where I spend my holiday."

In The Shade Of The Old Apple Tree

Words & Music by Egbert Van Alstyne & Harry Williams

The 1905 hit 'In The Shade Of The Old Apple Tree' was originally a success for Charles Holland in music hall days. Its composer, Boston born Egbert Van Alstyne, became a song plugger in New York where he teamed up with Harry Williams. They worked together as a vaudeville team singing their hits - including this one.

way, I can't for-get the way I once ca - rassed you;____ I

on - ly pray we'll meet an - oth - er day.____ In the

Valse lento

shade of the old ap - ple tree,____ where the

love in your eyes I could see,____ when the

voice that I heard, like the song of the bird, seem'd to

whis - per sweet mu - sic to me; I could

hear the dull buzz of the bee, in the

blos - soms as you said to me, with a

Verse 2:
I've really come a long way from the city
And though my heart is breaking I'll be brave
I've brought this bunch of flow'rs I think they're pretty
To place upon a freshly moulded grave;

If you will show me, father, where she's lying
Or if it's far just point it out to me
Said he "She told us all when she was dying
To bury her beneath the apple tree."

Leslie Stuart (real name Thomas Augustine Barratt) from Southport, Lancashire, wrote 'Little Dolly Daydream' for blackface singer Eugene Stratton in 1897 and achieved similar success with 'Lily Of Laguna' and his score for the extremely successful musical comedy Florodora.

Little Dolly Daydream

Words & Music by Leslie Stuart

1. I've
(Verse 2 see block lyric)

wait - ed long to have ma say, till South - ern garls have

Verse 2:

I ain't spoke yet, nor her to me
But lor! ye purty soon can see
She's only waitin' for me statin'
Dat I'm just as much in lub as she.

Dere's one poor cuss, she fools him so
He tells dem all round Idaho
Dat he's her best intended
Bekase deir styles has blended
But she fools wid him to send my jealous on de go.

Love's Old Sweet Song

Words by J. Clifton Bingham
Music by James L. Molloy

'Love's Old Sweet Song', also known by the first line of its chorus 'Just A Song At Twilight', was written by the Irish composer James Lyman Molloy, who studied law and was appointed secretary to the Attorney General. Although born in 1835, he wrote his first song in 1863. This one dates from 1884 and is the most popular. It was introduced by Annette Sterling.

1. Once in the dear, dead days be-yond re - call, when on the world the
(Verse 2 see block lyric)

mists be-gan to fall, out of the dreams that rose in hap-py throng,

low to our hearts love sang an old sweet song, and in the dusk where

fell the fire-light gleam, soft-ly it wove it-self in-to our dream.

Just a song at twi-light, when the lights are

low; and the flick-'ring shad-ows,

soft-ly come and go. Tho' the heart be

wea - ry.   sad the day and long,

still to us at twi - - - light comes love's old

song,   comes   love's___ old   sweet_____ song.

Verse 2:
Even today we hear love's song of yore
Deep in our hearts it swells forever-more
Foorsteps may falter
Weary grow the way
Still we can hear it at the close of day
So 'til the end when life's dim shadows fall
Love will be found the sweetest song of all.

Nellie Dean

Words & Music by Harry Armstrong

Andante moderato

1. By the old mill stream I'm dream-ing, Nel - lie
(Verse 2 see block lyric)

Dean, dream-ing of your bright eyes gleam-ing, Nel - lie Dean. As they

Verse 2:
I recall the day we parted, Nellie Dean
How you trembled, broken hearted, Nellie Dean
And you pinned a rose of red
On my coat of blue and said
That a soldier boy you'd wed, Nellie Dean.

All the world seems sad and lonely, Nellie Dean
For I love you and you only, Nellie Dean.
And I wonder if on high
You still love me if you sigh
For the happy days are gone by, Nellie Dean.

The Man Who Broke The Bank At Monte Carlo

Words & Music by Fred Gilbert

For - tune smil'd up - on me as she'd nev - er done be - fore, and I've

now such lots of mo - ney, I'm a gent. Yes, I've

now such lots of mo - ney, I'm a gent. As I

walk a - long the *Bois Boo - long*, with an in - de - pen - dent air, you can

Verse 2:

I stay indoors till after lunch, and then my daily walk
To the great Triumphal Arch is one grand Triumphal march
Observ'd by each observer with the keenness of a hawk
I'm a mass of money, linen, silk and starch.
I'm a mass of money, linen, silk and starch.

Verse 3:

I patronized the tables at the Monte Carlo hell
Till they hadn't got a sou for a Christian or a Jew
So I quickly went to Paris for the charms of mad'moiselle
Who's the loadstone of my heart – What can I do
When with twenty tongues she swears that she'll be true?

Sweet Genevieve

Words & Music by George Cooper & Henry Tucker

There's no connection between this 1869 song by George Cooper and Henry Tucker and the film about the Brighton Old Crocks Road Race. The lyrics of our song were written to commemorate the early death, just after their marriage, of Cooper's wife Genevieve. It was featured in the film Incendiary Blonde starring Betty Hutton.

Slow with expression

1. O Ge - ne - vieve, I'd give the world to
(Verse 2 see block lyric)

live a - gain the love - ly past! The rose of youth is

dew - im-pearl'd, but now it with - ers in the blast. I

days may come, the days— may go, but still the hands of

mem - 'ry weave the bliss - ful dreams of long a - go.

Verse 2:
Fair Genevieve, my early love!
The years but make thee dearer far
My heart shall never, never rove
Thou art my only guiding star.

For me the past has no regret
Whate'er the years may bring to me
I bless the hour when first we met
The hour that gave me love and thee!

George Bastow and F. W. Leigh wrote the catchy 'Galloping Major' that hymned the joys of equestrianism. It was sung and performed by music hall artist Harry Fay and subsequently was taken up by radio comedian Jack Train. It was also the title song for a comedy film starring Basil Radford.

The Galloping Major

Words & Music by G. Bastow & F. W. Leigh

1. When I was in the ar-my I was a cav-al-ry man, you
(Verses 2 & 3 see block lyric)

know,_____ and when-ev-er I went on pa-rade_____ a mag-

46

Verse 2:

Last year I thought I'd treat myself to a holiday by the sea
So I went, and my quarters I fixed
Then I found that the bathing was mixed.
So I gallop'd away to a bathing machine
In the busiest part of the day
And I soon felt at home with the girls in the water
And join'd in their frivolous play.
They were beautiful creatures, but lor!
How they giggled as soon as they saw *me*

Verse 3:

I always was a ladies man and a favourite with the sex
Well, I called upon one yesterday
Though I won't give the lady away.
She started to talk of my army career
And was quite interested, you see
But I got rather tired, so we talk'd about her
Which was more interesting to me.
And she said I'd been taking some wine
For as soon as we sat down to dine *I went*

Waiting At The Church

Words & Music by Fred Leigh & Henry Pether

'Can't get away to marry you today - my wife won't let me!' - the final revelatory twist in one of the most popular of all music hall songs was another smash hit for the beloved Vesta Victoria. It was written in 1906 and had a welcome revival in the Bing Crosby/Mary Martin picture The Birth Of The Blues.

1. I'm in a nice bit of trou-ble, I con-fess;

(Verses 2 & 3 see block lyric)

some-bo-dy with me has had a game. I should by now be a

Verse 2:
Lor, what a fuss Obadiah made of me
When he used to take me in the park!
He used to squeeze me till I was black and blue
When he kissed me he used to leave a mark.

Each time he met me he treated me to port
Took me now and then to see the play
Understand me rightly, when I say he treated me
It wasn't *him* but *me* that used to pay.

Verse 3:
Just think of how disappointed I must feel
I'll be off my crumpet very soon.
I've lost my husband the one I never had!
And I dreamed so about the honeymoon.

I'm looking out for another Obadiah
I've already bought the wedding ring
There's all my little fal-the-riddles packed up in my box–
Yes, absolutely two of ev'rything.

Where Did You Get That Hat?

Words & Music by Jos. J Sullivan

It may not be immediately obvious but composer Joseph Sullivan based his catchy song on themes from Wagner's Lohengrin and Die Meistersinger. The vaudeville artiste/composer, rummaging in an old trunk, found an old hat that caused much amusement. He introduced the song at the Miners Eighth Avenue Theater, New York in 1888.

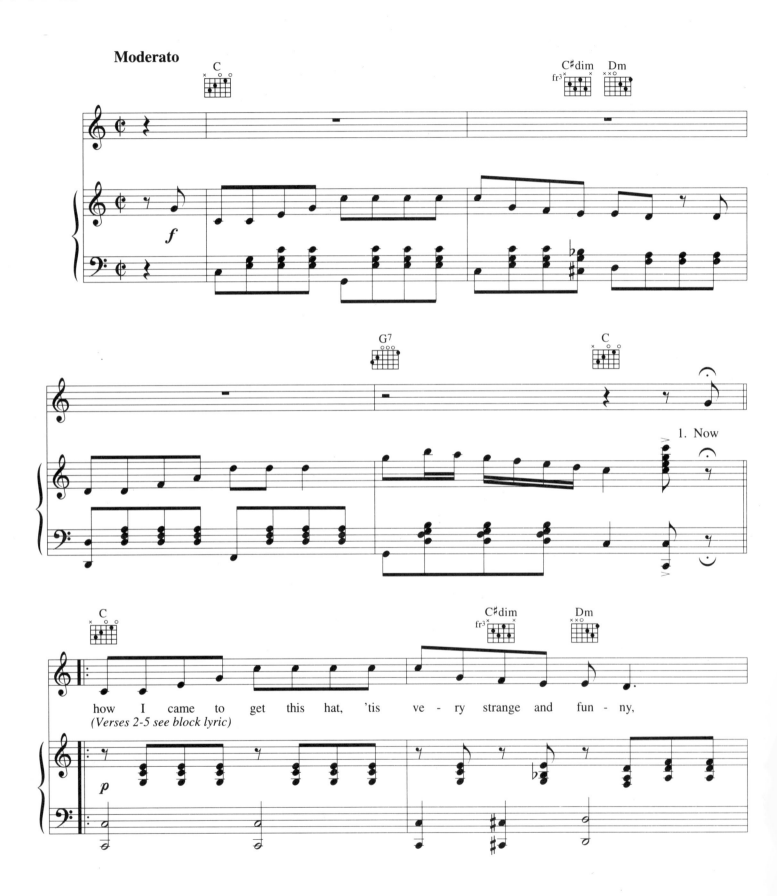

how I came to get this hat, 'tis ve-ry strange and fun-ny,

(Verses 2-5 see block lyric)

Grand-fa-ther died and left to me his pro-per-ty and mon-ey; and when the will it was read out, they told me straight and flat, if I would have his mon-ey I must al-ways wear his hat!

Chorus

'Where did you get that hat? Where did you get that tile? Is-n't it a nob-by one, and

just the pro-per style? I should like to have one just the same as that!' Where-

e'er I go they shout, 'Hel - lo! Where did you get that hat?' 2. If

Verse 2:
If I go to the op'rahouse, in the op'ra season
There's someone sure to shout at me without the slightest reason
If I go to a Concert Hall to have a jolly spree
There's someone in the party who is sure to shout at me:

Verse 3:
At twentyone I thought I would to my sweetheart get married
The people in the neighbourhood had said too long we'd tarried
So off to church we went right quick determined to get wed
I had not long been in there, when the parson to me said:

Verse 4:
I once tried hard to me be M.P., but failed to get elected
Upon a tub I stood, round which a thousand folks collected
And I had dodged the eggs and bricks (which was no easy task)
When one man cried, 'A question I the candidate would ask!'

Verse 5:
When Colonel South, the millionaire, gave his last garden party
I was amongst the guests who had a welcome true and hearty
The Prince of Wales was also there, and my heart jump'd with glee
When I was told the Prince would like to have a word with me.

Spoken after 1st verse. – And everywhere I go – everyone shouts after me –
Spoken after 4th verse. – I told him that I was ready to reply to any question that could be put to me. The man said – "Thousands of
British working people are anxiously awaiting enlightenment on the subject on which I am about to address
you. It is a question of national importance, in fact; THE great problem of the day – and that is, Sir –
Spoken after 5th verse. – I was duly presented to His Royal Highness, who immediately exclaimed –

Wot Cher!
(Knock'd 'Em In The Old Kent Road)

Words & Music by Charles Ingle

No wonder the 'Coster's Laureate', celebrated music hall performer Albert Chevalier, shortened his name. His middle names were Onesime Britannicus Gwatheveoyd Louis and he was born in Notting Hill in 1861. His brother Auguste was his manager and wrote songs under the name Charles Ingle - including this famous ditty, knocked up one Sunday morning.

Verse 2:

Some says nasty things about the moke
One cove thinks 'is leg is really broke
That's 'is envy, cos we're carriage folk
Like the toffs as rides in Rotten Row!
Straight! It woke the alley up a bit
Thought our lodger would 'ave 'ad a fit
When my missus, who's a real wit
Says "I 'ates a Bus because it's low!"

Verse 3:

When we starts the blessed donkey stops
He won't move, so out I quickly 'ops
Pals start whackin' him, when down he drops
Someone says he wasn't made to go.
Lor it might 'ave been a four in 'and
My old Dutch knows 'ow to do the grand
First she bows, and then she waves 'er 'and
Calling out we're goin' for a blow!

Verse 4:

Ev'ry evenin' on the stroke of five
Me and missus takes a little drive
You'd say, "Wonderful they're still alive"
If you saw that little donkey go.
I soon showed him that 'e'd have to do
Just whatever he was wanted to
Still I shan't forget that rowdy crew,
'Ollerin' "Woa! steady! Neddy Woa!"

Ah! Sweet Mystery Of Life

Music by Victor Herbert
Words by Rida Johnson Young

hopes, the joy and i-dle tears that fall!_____ For 'tis love, and love a-lone, the world is

seek - ing; And 'tis love, and love a-lone, that can re - pay, 'tis the

ans - wer, 'tis the end and all of liv - ing,_____ for it is

love a - lone that rules for aye! For 'tis

Alexander's Ragtime Band

Words & Music by Irving Berlin

First sung by Eddie Miller and Helen Vincent at the Garden Cafe in New York in 1911, 'Alexander's Ragtime Band' was an early hit for composer Irving Berlin. It was sung by Ethel Merman in the film of the same name - and Johnie Ray in There's No Business Like Show Business, Britain first heard the song in the revue Hello Ragtime, which starred Lew Hearn and Shirley Kellogg.

1. Oh, ma hon - ey, oh, ma hon - ey, bet - ter hur - ry and
(Verse 2 see block lyric)

hear,_____ come on and hear,_____ Al - ex - an - der's rag - time

band,_____ come on and hear,_____ come on and hear,_____ it's the

best band in the land,_____ they can play a bu - gle call like you

nev - er heard be - fore, so nat - ur - al that you want to go to war,

that's just the best - est band that am,

hon - ey lamb; come on a - long,_____ come on a - long,_____ let me

take you by the hand,_____ up to the man,_____ up to the

man_____ who's the lead - er of the band,_____ and if you

Verse 2:
Oh, ma honey, oh, ma honey
There's a fiddle with notes that screeches
Like a chicken, like a chicken
And the clarinet, is a colored pet
Come and listen, come and listen
To a classical band what's peaches
Come now, some how
Better hurry along.

Any Old Iron

Music by Charles Collins
Words by Fred Terry & A. E. Sheppard

1. Just a week or two a-go my poor old Un-cle Bill, went and kick'd the buck-et and he
(*Verses 2 - 4 see block lyric*)

left me in his will. The oth-er day I popp'd a-round to see poor Aun-tie Jane, she

said "Your Unc - le Bill has left to you a watch and chain." I put it on right a - cross my vest, thought I look'd a dan - dy as it dan - gled on my chest. Just to flash it off I start - ed walk - ing round a - bout, a lot of kid - dies foll - ow'd me and all be - gan to shout:

"A - ny old iron, a - ny old iron, a - ny, a - ny old, old i - ron? You look neat, talk a - bout a treat, you look dap - per from your nap - per to your feet. Dress'd in style, brand new tile, and your fath - er's old green tie on, but I

Verse 2:
I went to the City once and thought I'd have a spree
The Mayor of London, he was there, that's who I went to see
He dashed up in a canter, with a carriage and a pair
I shouted "Holler boys" and threw my hat up in the air.

Just then the Mayor he began to smile
Saw my face and then he shouted "Lummy what a dial!"
Started a Lord Mayoring and I thought that I should die
When pointing to my watch and chain he holler'd to me "Hi!"

Verse 3:
Just to have a little bit of fun the other day
Made up in my watch and chain I went and drew my pay
Then got out with a lot of other Colonels "on the loose"
I got full right up to here in fourp'ny "stagger juice."

One of them said "We want a pot of ale
"Run him to the ragshop, and we'll bung him on the scale"
I heard the fellow say "What's in this bundle that you've got"
Then whisper to me kindly: "Do you want to lose your lot?"

Verse 4:
Shan't forget when I got married to Selina Brown
The way the people laugh'd at me, it made me feel a clown
I began to wonder, when their dials began to crack
If by mistake I'd got my Sunday trousers front to back.

I wore my chain on my darby kell
The sun was shining on it and it made me look a swell
The organ started playing and the bells began to ring
My chain began to rattle, so the choir began to sing.

Fred Murray wrote this splendidly unsubtle music hall success in 1910. It was both sung and recorded by Harry Champion, born in Shoreditch and always a full blooded performer, who specialised in singing his songs at terrific speed. He continued to perform right into his seventies.

Ginger, You're Balmy

Words & Music by Fred Murray

1. I'm al-ways in the fash-ion, I'm a not-ed chap for that, so
(Verses 2 & 3 see block lyric)

late-ly I've been walk-ing a-bout the streets with-out a hat. I do with-out a ca-dy, and it

saves me half a quid. I'm like a bloom - ing sauce - pan on the fire with-out a lid.

I go you know, strol - ling round the town, and wag my lit - tle cane a -

- bout. Girls they all say "Gin - ger's on the mash!" Then

dig me in the ribs and loud - ly shout,

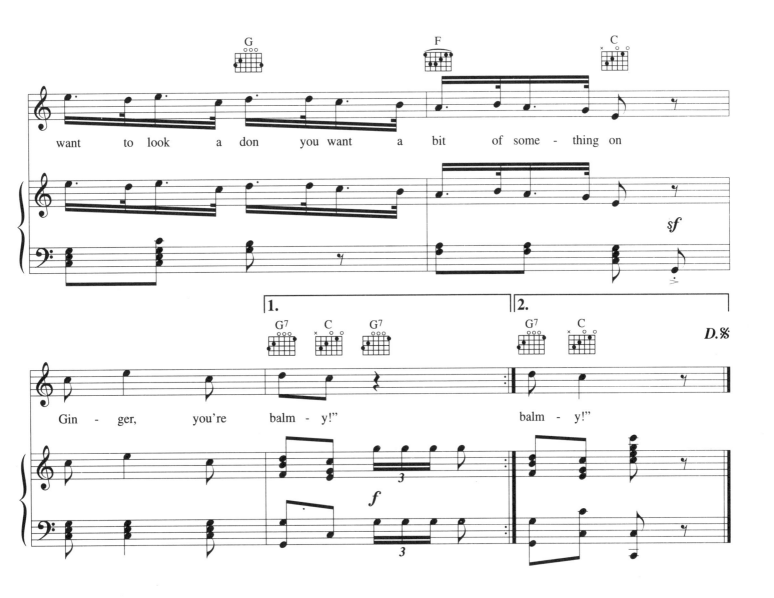

want to look a don you want a bit of some - thing on

Gin - ger, you're balm - y!" balm - y!"

D.%

Verse 2:

One day I went into the zoo with such a smiling face
But, oh! there was a hullabaloo when I got in the place
The keeper started chasing me, though I was in a rage
They put a chain around my neck and bunged me in a cage.

I cried, "I'm not a monkey, on my word!"
Then I had to buy them all some beer
When they let me out they told me this
"If you want to keep away from here:"

Verse 3:

My missus took me in a pub; the guv'nor, Mister Hogg
He stroked my head and gave me a cake, he took me for a dog
A p'liceman stopped the traffic, shouted out with all his might
"Look out! here comes the North Pole with the top part all alight."

My wife said, "Your napper's like a sieve
"It's full of little holes I bet!
"When it rains 'twill let the water in
"And then your feet will both of 'em get wet."

Lily Of Laguna

Words & Music by Leslie Stuart

Leslie Stuart wrote his greatest success for the blackface singer Eugene Stratton (a precursor of Al Jolson) who first performed 'Lily Of Laguna' at the Oxford Music Hall in 1898. Laguna, according to its composer, is on the road from New Orleans to California, a hundred miles to the left. Errol Flynn sang the ditty in Lilacs In The Spring. The original lyrics to this song may be considered racially insensitive; however, they have been included for historical authenticity.

1. It's de same old tale of a pal-pa-ta-ting nig-gar ev-'ry
(Verse 2 see block lyric)

time, ev-'ry time; it's de same old

wait - in' for de sig - nal of ma lit - tle la - dy love.

She's ma la - dy love, _____ she is ma dove, ma

ba - by love, she's no gal for sit - tin' down to dream,

she's de on - ly queen La - gu - na knows; I know she

Verse 2:

When I first met Lil it was down in old Laguna at de dance, oder night
So she says, "Say, a'm curious for to know
"When ye leave here de way yer goin' to go
"'Kase a wants to see who de lady is dat claims ye all way home, way home tonight."

I says, "I've no gal, never had one,"
And den ma Lilly, ma Lilly, ma Lilly gal!
She says, kern't believe ye, a kern't believe ye
Else I'd like to have ye shapperoon me.

Dad says he'll esscortch me, says he'll esscortch me
But it's mighty easy for to lose him"
Since then each sun down I wander down here and roam around
Until I know ma lady wants me
Till I hear de music ob de signal sound.

Moonlight Bay

Music by Percy Wenrich
Words by Edward Madden

Percy Wenrich from Joplin, Massachusetts started by playing in saloons and bars and sold his own self published compositions door-to-door. He subsequently wrote for many Broadway shows and married singer Dolly Connolly. He was 32 when he wrote one of his big hits 'Moonlight Bay', sung by Alice Faye in Tin Pan Alley and Doris Day in a film named for the song.

Verse 2:
Candle lights gleaming on the silent shore
Lonely nights, dreaming till we meet once more.
Far apart, her heart is yearning
With a sigh for my returning
With the light of love still burning
As in days of yore.

Oh! You Beautiful Doll

Words & Music by Seymour Brown & Nat D. Ayer

An early (1911) hit for American born Nat D. Ayer was 'Oh! You Beautiful Doll', which he wrote before coming to Britain, in partnership with A. Seymour Brown. It became the melody of car horns in the 1920s, was the title tune of a 40s film and was danced to by Fred Astaire and Ginger Rogers in the biographical film The Story Of Vernon And Irene Castle.

1. Hon-ey dear,— want you near,— just turn out the light and then come
(Verse 2 see block lyric)

ov-er here;— nes-tle close— up to my side,—

my heart's a - fire with love's de - sire.

In my arms rest com - plete, I

nev - er thought that life could ev - er be so sweet till I met you

some time a - go, but now you know

I love you so.

Oh! you beau-ti-ful doll,— you great big beau-ti-ful doll!—

Let— me put my arms a-bout you, I— could nev-er live with-out you,

Oh! you beau-ti-ful doll,— you great big beau-ti-ful doll!— If you

Verse 2:
Precious prize, close your eyes
Now we're goin' to visit lover's paradise
Press your lips again to mine
For love is king of ev'rything.

Squeeze me, dear, I don't care!
Hug me just as if you were a grizzly bear
This is how I'll go thro' life
No care or strife when you're my wife.

Memphis Blues

Words & Music by W. C. Handy

© Copyright 1913 Theron C. Bennett, USA.
© Copyright 1916 Assigned to Joe Morris Company, USA.
Campbell Connelly & Company Limited, 8/9 Frith Street, London W1.
All Rights Reserved. International Copyright Secured.

could-n't spend— a dime, had the grand - est time, I went out a-dance - in' with a Ten - nes - see dear,— a fel - low there nam'd Han - dy had a band you should hear,— while they gent - ly swayed, all them dark - ies played real— har - mon - y.— I nev - er will for - get— the tune that Han - dy called the Mem-phis

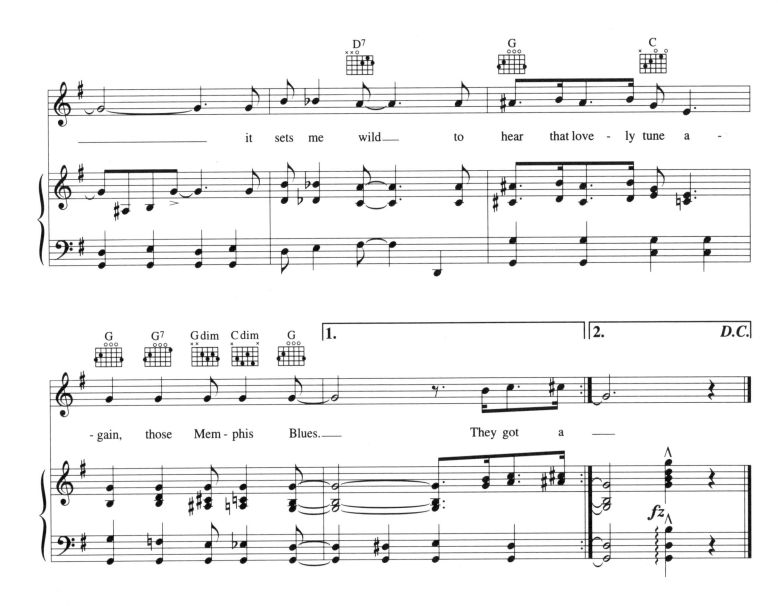

it sets me wild___ to hear that love - ly tune a - gain, those Mem - phis Blues.___ They got a ___

Verse 2:
Oh, that melody sure appeals to me
Like a mountain stream, flowing on it seem'd
Then it slowly died, with a gentle sigh
As the breeze that whines in the summer pines
Hear me people, hear me people, hear me, I pray
I'll take a million lessons till I learn how to play
Seems I hear it yet, simply can't forget, that blue refrain
There's nothing like the Handy Band
That plays the Memphis Blues so grand, oh them blues.

Don't Dilly Dally On The Way

Words & Music by Fred W. Leigh & Charles Collins

The composer of 'Any Old Iron',
Charles Collins, combined with the lyricist
of 'Waiting At The Church', Fred Leigh,
to write in 1915 the definitive song about
moving house which became a favourite of
the queen of the music hall, Marie Lloyd.
It is also known by its first line –
'My Old Man Said "Follow The Van"'.

had to move a-way, 'cos the rent we could-n't pay, the

(Verses 2 & 3 see block lyrics)

got in - side all we could get in - side,_____ then we

packed all we could pack on the tail - board at the back, till there

was - n't a - ny room for me to ride._____

My old man said, "Fol - low the van, don't dil - ly

dal - ly on the way!" _____ Off went the cart with the

home packed in it, I walked be - hind with my old cock

lin - net. But I dil - lied and dal - lied, dal - lied and dil - lied,

lost the van and don't know where to roam. _____

1. I
2. Now
3. You

fz *p*

stopp'd on the way to have the old half - quart - ern, and I can't find
who's go - ing to put up the old iron bed - stead, if I can't find
can't trust the "spe-cials" like the old - time "cop-pers" when you can't find

1.

my way home.
my way home?
your way home.

2. *D.%.*

home._____
home?_____
home._____

Verse 2:

I gave a helping hand with the marble wash-hand-stand,
And straight, we wasn't getting on so bad
All at once the carman bloke had an accident and broke
Well, the nicest bit of china that we had.

You'll understand of course, I was cross about the loss
Same as any other human woman would
But I soon got over that, what with "two-out" and a chat
'Cos it's little things like that what does you good.

Verse 3:

Oh! I'm in such a mess– I don't know the new address–
Don't even know the blessed neighbourhood
And I feel as if I might have to stay out all the night
And that ain't a-goin' to do me any good.

I don't make no complaint, but I'm coming over faint
What I want now is a good substantial feed
And I sort o' kind o' feel, if I don't soon have a meal
I shall have to rob the linnet of his seed.

Although it sounds like an authentic Irish ballad, 'I'll Take You Home Again Kathleen' was written in either Indiana or Kentucky (the composer moved around a lot) by Thomas P. Westendorf. He wrote the song to comfort his wife who wanted to return to the East Coast. Her name, incidentally, was Jennie!

I'll Take You Home Again Kathleen

Words & Music by Thomas P. Westendorf

Andante con espressione

1. I'll take you home a - gain, Kath -
(Verses 2 & 3 see block lyrics)

- leen, a - cross the o - cean wild and wide, to

where your heart has ev - er been, since first you were my bon - ny bride. The ro - ses all have left your cheek, I've watched them fade a - way and die; your voice is sad when-e'er you speak, and tears be - dim your lov - ing eyes. Oh!

Verse 2:

I know you love me, Kathleen dear
Your heart was ever fond and true
I always feel when you are near
That life holds nothing dear but you.

The smiles that once you gave to me
I scarcely ever see them now
Though many, many times I see
A dark'ning shadow on your brow.

Verse 3:

To that dear home beyond the sea
My Kathleen shall again return
And when thy old friends welcome thee
Thy loving heart will cease to yearn.

Where laughs the little silver stream
Beside your mother's humble cot
And brightest rays of sunshine gleam
There all your grief will be forgot.

If You Were The Only Girl In The World

Music by Nat D. Ayer
Words by Clifford Grey

American composer Nat D. Ayer came to Britain with the American Ragtime Octette in 1910 and stayed on to write a stream of hits. In 1916 he wrote 'If You Were The Only Girl In The World' for the London revue The Bing Boys Are Here, starring Violet Loraine. It has remained one of the most beloved of all show songs.

call　　　my　　　own.＿＿＿＿＿＿＿＿＿　If

very slow with expression

{ you / I } were the on - - ly girl in the world, and

I / you were the on - - ly boy,＿＿＿＿＿＿＿

noth - ing else would mat - ter in the world to - day,

we could go on lov - ing in the same old way. A

Gar - den of E - den just made for two, with

noth - ing to mar our joy,

I would say such won-der-ful things to you,

MacNamara's Band

Words by John J. Stamford
Music by Shamus O'Connor

1. My name is Mac-na-ma-ra, I'm the lead-er of the band, and tho' we're small in num-ber we're the best in all the land! Oh!

105

2. When - ev - er an e -
(Verse 3 see block lyric)

- lec - tion's on we play on ei - ther side._____ The way we play our

fine ould airs fills Ir - ish hearts with pride, oh! if poor Tom Moore was

liv - ing now, he'd make yez un - der - stand_____ that none could do him

jus - tice like ould "Mac - na - ma - ra's band." When the drums go bang, the cym - bals clang, the

horns will blaze a - way,_____ Mac - Car - thy puffs the ould bas - soon while Doyle the pipes will

play; Oh! Hen - nes - sy Ten - nes - sy too - tles the flute, my word 'tis some - thing

grand, oh! a cred - it to ould Ire - land, boys, is Mac - na - ma - ra's band! Tra - la - la

Verse 3:
We play at wakes and weddings, and at ev'ry county ball
And at any great man's funeral we play the "Dead March in Saul"
When the Prince of Wales to Ireland came, he shook me by the hand
And said he'd never heard the like of "Macnamara's band."

Why Am I Always The Bridesmaid?

Words & Music by Charles Collins & Fred W. Leigh

© Copyright 1917 Francis Day & Hunter Limited, 127 Charing Cross Road, London WC2.
All Rights Reserved. International Copyright Secured.

A classic music hall song written for music hall star Lily Morris, who portrayed an indomitable char, by the reliable team of Clarles Collins and Fred Leigh. Many music hall stars refused to record their greatest hits, lest others copy them. Not so Lily Morris. She recorded her interpretation of the song both on film and gramophone record.

Repeat until ready

1. Why am I dressed in these beau - ti - ful clothes?
(Verses 2 & 3 see block lyrics)

p colla voce

What is the mat - ter with me?

I've been the brides - maid for twen - ty - two brides,

this time - 'll make twen - ty - three.

Twen - ty - two la - dies I've helped off the shelf,

no doubt it seemd a bit strange.

be - ing the brides - maid is no good to me, and I
think I could do with a change.
Why am I al - ways the brides - - - maid, nev - er the
blush - ing bride? Ding - - - dong!

wed - ding bells on - ly ring for oth - er

'gels, but some fine day

Oh, let it be soon! I shall wake up

in the morn - ing on my own hon - ey -

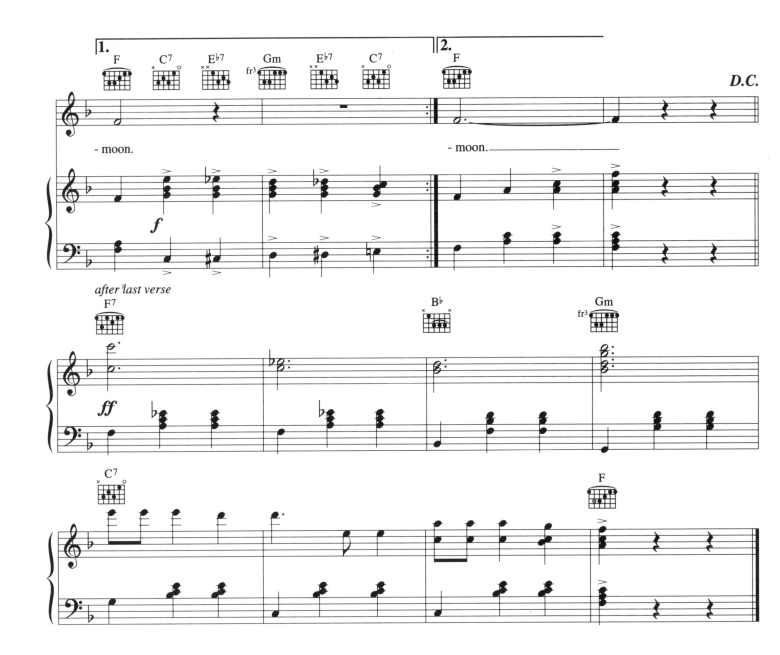

D.C.

Verse 2:

Twenty-two times have I gone to the church
Followed the bride up the aisle
Twenty-two ladies have answered "I will"
Meaning "I won't" all the while.

Twenty-two couples I've seen go away
Just him and her on their own
Twenty-two times I have wished it was me
And gone back home to Mother alone.

Verse 3:

I had a good chance a week or two back
Took my young man home to tea
Mother got playful and gave him a pinch
Pinched my "financy" from me.

Being a widow she knew what to do
No use for me to complain
When they got married today, if you please
I was only the bridesmaid again.

Blues My Naughty Sweetie Gives To Me

Words & Music by Arthur N. Swanstrom,
Charles R. McGarron & Carey Morgan

Although a prolific songwriter, Arthur Swanstrom's greatest and most enduring hit was 'Blues My Naughty Sweetie Gives To Me', written in cahoots with Charles R. McGarron and Carey Morgan. From its first appearance in 1919 it quickly became a jazz standard, memorably recorded by Jimmy Noone and Ted Lewis and his orchestra.

1. What is that song— a-bout kiss-es?— What is that song— a-bout

(Verse 2 see block lyric)

smiles? If I could have— my way, I'd sing a song— to-day,

that would beat them all by miles, I would-n't sing— a-bout

smil - ing,——— that's not the ti - tle I'd choose,

I would sing— a-bout what I've got,— and what I've got's the wea-ry blues. There are

(Chorus 2 & 3 see block lyrics)

blues_____ that you get from wor - ry,_____ there are

blues_____ that you get from pain,_____ and there are

blues when you're lone - 'ly, for your one and on - ly, the

blues you can nev - er ex - plain,_____ there are

blues my naugh - ty swee - tie gives —— to me.

There are me. ———

Chorus 2:

There are blues that you get when single
Those are blues that will give you pain
And there are blues when you're lonely
For your one and only
The blues you can never explain
There are blues that you get from longing
To hold someone on your knee
But the kind of blues that always stabs
Comes from hiring taxicabs
The blues my naughty sweetie gives to me.

Verse 2:

No use in chasing those rainbows
Rainbows will never help you
They look so bright and gay
But they will fade away
Then you'll find the sky's all blue
Look at the ocean and that's blue
My sweetie's eyes are blue too
When she got me she blew away
And natur'ly that makes me blue.

Chorus 3:

There are blues that you get from sweetie
When she 'phones to another guy
And there are blues when your honey
Spends all of your money
And blues when she tells you a lie
There are blues that you get when married
Wishing that you could be free
But the kind of blues that's good and blue
Comes from buying wine for two
The kind of blues my sweetie gives to me.

Your King And Country Want You

Words & Music by Paul A. Rubens

Tempo di marcia

rather slowly and quite simply

1. We've watched you play - ing cric - ket and ev - 'ry kind of game at
(Verses 2 & 3 see block lyric)

foot - ball, golf and po - lo, you men have made your name, but now your coun - try calls you to

play your part in war, and no mat-ter what be-falls you, we shall love you all the more, so,

come and join the for-ces as your fa-thers did be-fore. Oh! we

don't want to lose you but we think you ought to go, for your

King and your Coun-try both need you so; we shall

* When used for Male Voice substitue the word "bless" for kiss.

Verse 2:
We want you from all quarters
So, help us, South and North
We want you in your thousands
From Falmouth to the Forth
You'll never find us fail you
When you are in distress
So, answer when we hail you
And let your word be "yes"
And so your name, in, years to come
Each mother's son shall bless.

Encore Verse
It's easy for us women/people
To stay at home and home and shout
But remember, there's a duty
To the men who *first* went out
The odds against that handful
Were nearly four to one
And we cannot rest until
It's man for man, and gun for gun!
And ev'ry woman's/body's duty
Is to see that duty done!

* When used for Male Voices substitute the word "bless" for kiss.

Baby Won't You Please Come Home

Words & Music by Charles Warfield & Clarence Williams.

When you left you broke my heart ____ Be-
cause I nev - er thought we'd part. Ev - 'ry hour in the day, ___ you will
hear me say, ___ Ba - by won't you please come home.
home. Dad - dy needs mam - ma, Ba - by won't you please come home. ____

Show Me The Way To Go Home

Words & Music by Irving King.

Irving King is remembered today for just one song - 'Show Me The Way To Go Home', made famous in the early years of the century by male impersonator Ella Shields. The song has come to be associated with gentlemen who have drunk not wisely but too well. There are memorable recorded versions, by Michael Holliday and The Andrews Sisters.

128

Amapola

Words by Albert Gamse. Music by Joseph M. Lacalle.

Lyricist Haven Gillespie and composer Egbert Van Alstyne were responsible for many hits. Gillespie wrote 'Santa Claus Is Coming To Town', and 'Breezin' Along With The Breeze'. Van Alstyne composed 'In The Shade Of The Old Apple Tree' and 'Memories'. Together they co-wrote 'Drifting And Dreaming' in 1925. The song has been recorded by Vera Lynn, Bing Crosby and Nelson Riddle.

Drifting And Dreaming
(Sweet Paradise)

Words by Haven Gillespie. Music by Egbert Van Alstyne,
Erwin R. Schmidt & Loyal Curtis.

135

Baby Face

Words & Music by Harry Akst & Benny Davis.

Harry Akst scored a major hit with 'Baby Face', written in 1926 with Benny Davis and taken up by Al Jolson, who sang it in his second film biography, Jolson Sings Again, in 1949. In 1929 the song had cropped up in a part-Technicolor musical Glorifying The American Girl. In 1967 Julie Andrews sang it in the film musical Thoroughly Modern Millie

Ros - y cheeks and turn'd up nose and curl - y hair, _____ I'm rav - ing

'bout my ba - by now, _____ Pret - ty lit - tle dim - ples here and

dim - ples there; _____ Don't want to live with - out her, I love her good - ness

knows, I wrote a song a-bout her And here's the way it goes:

CHORUS

Ba - by Face, ___ You've got the cut-est lit - tle

Ba - by Face, ___ There's not an - oth - er one could take your place. ___

___ Ba - by Face, ___ my poor heart ___ is jump - in',

You sure have start - ed some-thin', Ba - by Face; ___ I'm up in

heav - en when I'm in your fond em - brace, _____ I did-n't

need a shove ___ 'Cause I just fell in love ___ with your pret - ty

Ba - by   Face. _____   Face. _____

Can't Help Lovin' Dat Man

Music by Jerome Kern. Words by Oscar Hammerstein II.

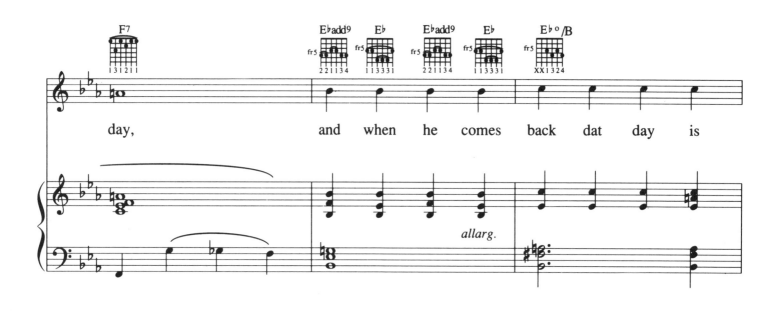

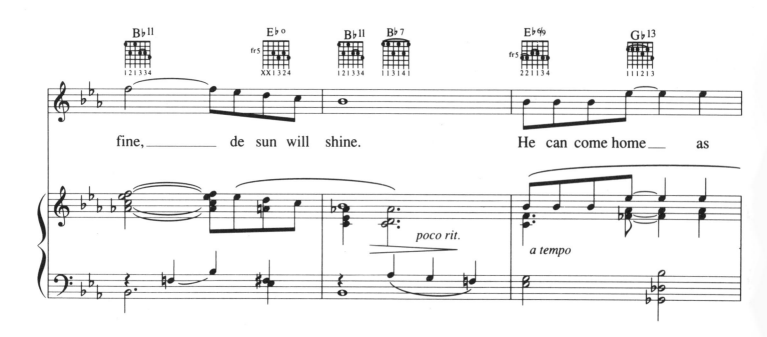

Ol' Man River

Music by Jerome Kern. Words by Oscar Hammerstein II.

One of the principal characters of the stage musical and film Show Boat is the Mississippi River, celebrated by Joe, played by Jules Bledsoe on Broadway and Paul Robeson in London - and on film. This 1927 song runs like a ribbon through the show and gave Jerome Kern and Oscar Hammerstein II one of their biggest hits, and Paul Robeson his signature tune.

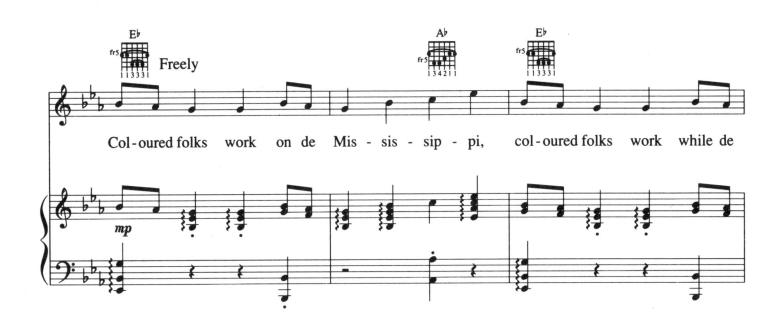

Col-oured folks work on de Mis - sis - sip - pi, col-oured folks work while de

white folks play. Pull-in' dose boats from de dawn to sun - set,

sick of try-in', Ah'm tired of liv-in' an' skeered of dy-in', but

ol' man riv-er, he jus' keeps roll-in' a - long.

long.

The Lonesome Road

Words by Gene Austin. Music by Nathaniel Shilkret.

The Broadway revue Blackbirds Of 1928 introduced one of the greatest of love songs, written by veteran composer Jimmy McHugh with one of the century's great lyricists, Dorothy Fields. She would go on to write classic songs with Jerome Kern, Arthur Schwartz and Cy Coleman. But it was 'I Can't Give You Anything But Love (baby)' that first revealed her fully formed talent.

I Can't Give You Anything But Love

Words by Dorothy Fields
Music by Jimmy McHugh

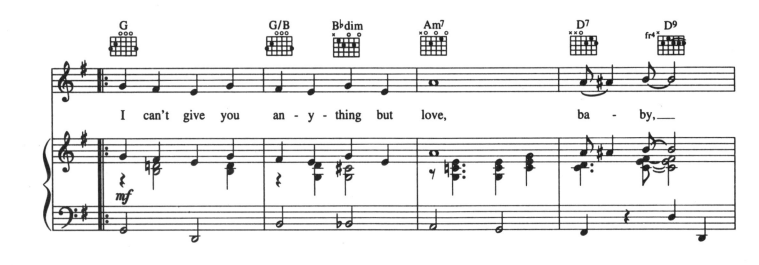

I can't give you an-y-thing but love, ba-by, ___

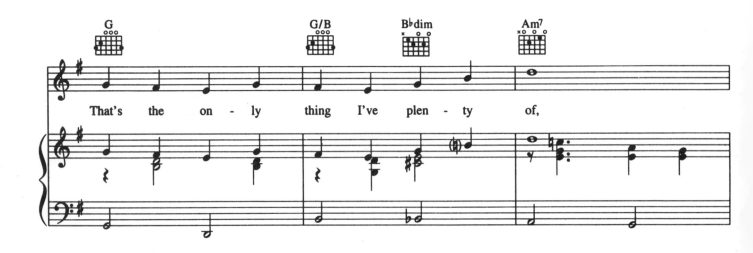

That's the on-ly thing I've plen-ty of,

152

Wool-worth does-n't sell, ba - by, Till that luck-y

day you know darn well, ba - by, ___

1. I can't give you an - y - thing but love.

2. I can't give you an - y - thing but love.

154

If I Had You

Words & Music by Ted Shapiro, Jimmy Campbell & Reg Connelly.

Ted Shapiro was Sophie Tucker's long-time accompanist, and wrote songs including 'If I Had You' (1929). His co-writers were the British publishing legends James Campbell and Reginald Connelly. Years later the song resurfaced in You Were Meant For Me, starring Jeanne Crain and Dan Dailey (1948) and also The Clock (1945) which starred Judy Garland.

155

157

Together

Words & Music by B.G. De Sylva, Lew Brown & Ray Henderson.

Buddy De Sylva, Lew Brown and Ray Henderson wrote many hits as a trio before De Sylva became a Hollywood producer. Their 1928 hit 'Together' was not written for any show, but was included in the biographical movies The Best Things In Life Are Free *and* Since You Went Away. *It was, however, sung on Broadway in* Good News, *in 1974, by Alice Faye.*

Moderately Slow

We strolled the lane, To-geth-er

Laughed at the rain, To-geth-er

Sang love's re-frain, To-geth-er. And we'd / We knew

That's My Weakness Now

Words & Music by Bud Green & Sam H. Stept.

Dream Lover

Words by Clifford Grey. Music by Victor Schertzinger.

bounds touch my room in the gloom, when the sha - dows creep.
wan - der en - rap - tured and whis - per sweet vows of love.

Some - one I met there waits for me, some - one
Not a cloud to dark - en our sky, not a

ten - der as a lov - er should be; And I whis - per each night as I
care we'll ev - er know, you and I; All the days will be fair with the

close my eyes in sleep. ——————— } Dream
sun - shine a - bove. ———————

lov - er fold your arms a - round me, dream

lov - er your ro - mance has found me, I'm

held in your spell, know - ing too well,

dreams nev - er tell. We

Honeysuckle Rose

Music by Thomas 'Fats' Waller. Words by Andy Razaf.

Thomas 'Fats' Waller was a larger-than-life entertainer, whose jolly, ebullient personality is immediately apparent from his songs, his piano playing and his singing. 'Honeysuckle Rose' was written with lyricist Andy Razaf and first published in 1929. There have been renowned performances from Coleman Hawkins, and from Lena Horne in the film Thousands Cheer.

Medium with a lift

Ev-'ry hon-ey bee fills with jeal-ous-y when they see you out with me, I don't blame them, good-ness knows,____ Hon-ey Suck-le Rose. When you're pass-in' by flow-ers droop and sigh, and I know the rea-son why, You're much sweet-er, good-ness knows,____

Miss You

Words by Charlie Tobias & Harry Tobias. Music by Henry M. Tobias.

that I still love you. Kiss you,___
in my dreams I kiss you,___ Whis - p'ring,___
"Dar-ling how I Miss You,"___ Tell me,___
do you ev-er miss me___ as I
Miss You. I You.___

From the stage show Great Day (1929)
came 'More Than You Know', written by
Vincent Youmans and Edward Eliscu
(with showman/impresario Billy Rose).
The song, a hit for Helen Morgan, was
featured in the film Hit The Deck and in
the second Barbra Streisand film about
Fanny Brice, Funny Lady (1975).

More Than You Know

Words by William Rose & Edward Eliscu.
Music by Vincent Youmans.

171

Herman (Harry) Ruby, Bud Green and Sam Stept wrote 'I'll Always Be In Love With You' in 1929. Two films included the song, Steppin' High and Syncopation. The latter featured Fred Waring, who recorded the song - as did Vera Lynn and Michael Holliday.

I'll Always Be In Love With You

Words & Music by Herman Ruby, Bud Green & Sam Stept.

Additional Verse (optional)
Sometimes when I'm all alone,
I keep wondering who is romancing with you.
How could I ever have known
I'd be broken hearted,
And now that we're parted.

(CHORUS)

Louise

Words by Leo Robin. Music by Richard A. Whiting.

Since he introduced the song in the 1929 film hit Innocents Of Paris, 'Louise' became the theme song of international film star Maurice Chevalier. It was written by Richard Whiting, father of popular singer Margaret Whiting, with celebrated lyricist Leo Robin. The film has long since vanished, but the song lives on.

Won-der-ful! Oh, it's won-der-ful, to be in love with you.
In-no-cent! You're as in-no-cent, and gen-tle as a dove.

Beau-ti-ful! You're so beau-ti-ful, you haunt me all day through.
Hea-ven sent! You were hea-ven sent, an an-gel from a-bove.

CHORUS

Ev-'ry lit-tle breeze seems to whis-per "Lou-ise." — Birds in the trees— seem to

Bye Bye Blues

Words & Music by Bert Lowe, Chauncey Gray, David Bennett & Fred Hamm.

Falling In Love Again

Music & Original Words by Friedrich Hollander.
English Words by Reg Connelly.

The Blue Angel *was the 1930 German film that brought international fame to Marlene Dietrich. Its decadent setting in the sleazy night-clubs of pre-war Germany was revolutionary in its time. The songs, by Friedrich Hollander, captured the world-weary cynicism of the time. And one - 'Falling in Love Again', with English words by Reg Connelly - became a standard.*

CHORUS

184

On The Sunny Side Of The Street

One of the happiest of all popular songs, 'On The Sunny Side Of The Street' is further testimony to the songwriting talent of Jimmy McHugh and Dorothy Fields. It surfaced in The International Revue on Broadway, and was soon snapped up for the movies - including Ted Lewis's Is Everybody Happy? as well as both The Benny Goodman Story and The Eddie Duchin Story.

Words by Dorothy Fields. Music by Jimmy McHugh.

Where The Blue Of The Night Meets The Gold Of The Day

Words & Music by Roy Turk, Fred Ahlert & Bing Crosby.

Bing Crosby was one of many stars of The Big Broadcast , a 1932 film musical revue. The plot concerned a failing radio station that was saved by the intervention of a series of stars. Bing co-wrote his own song 'Where The Blue Of The Night Meets The Gold Of The Day' and it became his signature tune. The other writers were lyricist Roy Turk and composer/arranger Fred E. Ahlert.

only I could see her,＿＿＿＿ oh, how hap - py

I would be!＿＿＿＿＿＿＿＿＿＿＿ Where the blue of the

night meets the gold of the day, some - one waits for

1. *rall.* me.＿＿＿＿＿＿＿ *a tempo* Where the **2.** *rall.* me.＿＿＿＿＿＿＿

Wrap Your Troubles In Dreams
(And Dream Your Troubles Away)

Words by Ted Koehler & Billy Moll. Music by Harry Barris.

Harry Barris, a former member of Paul Whiteman's vocal group The Rhythm Boys in the Twenties, appeared in many films, and led his own dance band. In 1931, with Ted Koehler and Billy Moll he created the song 'Wrap Your Troubles In Dreams'. It was featured in the films Top Man (1943) and Rainbow Round My Shoulder (1957), the latter featuring singing star Frankie Laine.

Underneath The Arches

Words & Music by Bud Flanagan.

'Underneath The Arches' was written by one half of the comedy duo (Bud) Flanagan and (Chesney) Allen. Both were seasoned musical performers before their first performance together in Birkenhead where they first performed their signature tune. It was used as the title song of their 1937 film, and was also the name of a successful tribute show just a few years ago.

The Ritz I nev-er sigh for, the Carl-ton they can keep, there's
I don't en-vy oth-ers the com-forts of a home, for

on-ly one place that I know, and that is where I sleep.
there's one place where I can rest, when I've no wish to roam.

CHORUS

Un-der-neath the

arch - es,_____ I dream my dreams a - way,_____ un - der - neath the

arch - es,_____ on cob - ble - stones I lay,_____ ev - 'ry night you'll

find me,_____ ti - red out and worn,_____ hap - py when the

day - light comes creep - ing, her - ald - ing the dawn. Sleep - ing when it's

rain - ing,____ and sleep-ing when it's fine,____ I hear the trains rat - tling

by a - bove,____ pave-ment is my pil - low,____ no mat-ter where I

stray,____ un-der-neath the arch-es, I dream my dreams a-

way. Un-der-neath the way.____

I'm Gettin' Sentimental Over You

Words by Ned Washington. Music by Geo. Bassman.

Ned Washington and George Bassman wrote 'I'm Gettin' Sentimental Over You' in 1932. Washington was a popular lyricist, contributing to stage and screen successes from the Twenties to the Sixties. Composer George Bassman was an arranger for films, and recordings. 'I'm Getting Sentimental Over You' was adopted as his signature tune by bandleader Tommy Dorsey.

Moderately slow

I was just an-oth-er who laughed at ro-mance, I said it was not for me.
Nev-er was a dream-er un-til I met you, fun-ny how one gets that way.

Then you made your en-trance and right at a glance, I knew this was meant for me.
Cu-pid's just a schem-er and I nev-er knew, now I'm dream-ing dreams all day.

CHORUS

Nev-er thought I'd fall, but now I hear love call, I'm get-ting sen-ti-men-tal ov-er you. Things you say and do, just thrill me thro' and thro', I'm get-ting sen-ti-men-tal ov-er you. I thought I was hap-py, I could live with-out

Don't Blame Me

Words & Music by Jimmy McHugh & Dorothy Fields.

Written in 1933, 'Don't Blame Me', by Dorothy Fields and Jimmy McHugh, was featured in MGM's Dinner at Eight with Jean Harlow, and Lionel and John Barrymore among its dinner guests. In 1979, the song made its Broadway début in the burlesque musical Sugar Babies, which starred Mickey Rooney and Ann Miller - who subsequently brought the show to London.

1. Ev-er since the luck-y night I found you___ I've hung a-round you,___ just like a fool

2. I like ev-'ry sin-gle thing a-bout you___ With-out a doubt you___ are like a dream.

Fall-ing head and heels in love like a kid out of

In my mind I find a pic-ture of us as a

how can I help it! Don't blame me! Can't you

see when you do the things you do! If I can't con-ceal, the

thrill that I'm feel-ing Don't blame me.

I can't help it if that dog-gone moon a-bove___

Stars Fell On Alabama

Words by Mitchell Parish. Music by Frank Perkins.

Salem, Massachusetts-born Frank Perkins was responsible for the music for a few choice songs. As a conductor/arranger, he lived in Hollywood, working on June Haver and Doris Day films. In 1934 he collaborated with Louisiana's Mitchell Parish on 'Stars Fell On Alabama'. The many recordings of this song include a classic by Billie Holiday.

Moon- light and mag- no - lia, star- light in your hair, all the world a dream come true,

did it real- ly hap- pen, was I real- ly there, was I real- ly there with you?

206

208

The Touch Of Your Lips

Words & Music by Ray Noble.

British bandleader Ray Noble was for many years Artists and Repertoire Manager for HMV, during which time he ran the finest studio-based dance band of all. During this time, and following his successful move to America, Noble found time to write some excellent songs. 'The Touch Of Your Lips' immediately became a standard with many fine recordings, notably one by Nat 'King' Cole.

Moderately Slow with expression

The

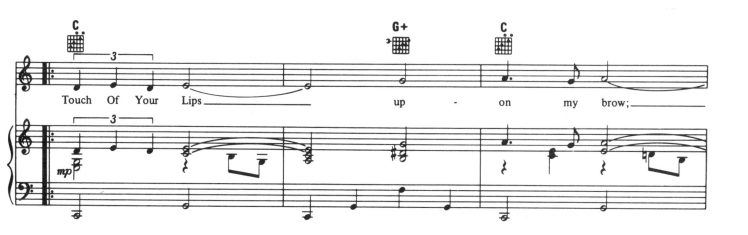

Touch Of Your Lips _____ up - on my brow; _____

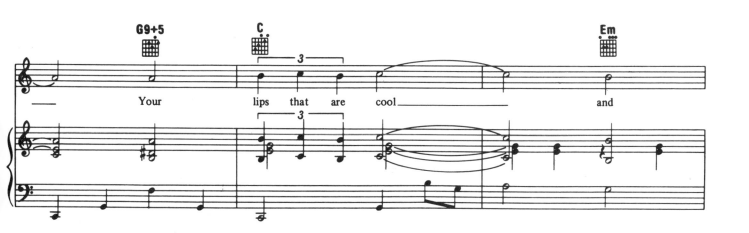

— Your lips that are cool _____ and

love in your eyes a - shine;

And now at last the mo - ment di -

vine, The Touch Of Your Lips on

mine. The mine. The mine.

East Of The Sun (And West Of The Moon)

Words & Music by Brooks Bowman

The film Pennies From Heaven was a 1936 charmer in which Bing Crosby befriended a little girl who had no home. There was a magnificent crop of songs and the title tune by Johnny Burke and Arthur Johnston was nominated for an Academy Award. In 1981 a second film of the same name was the film version of Dennis Potter's highly acclaimed television series.

Pennies From Heaven

Words by John Burke. Music by Arthur Johnston.

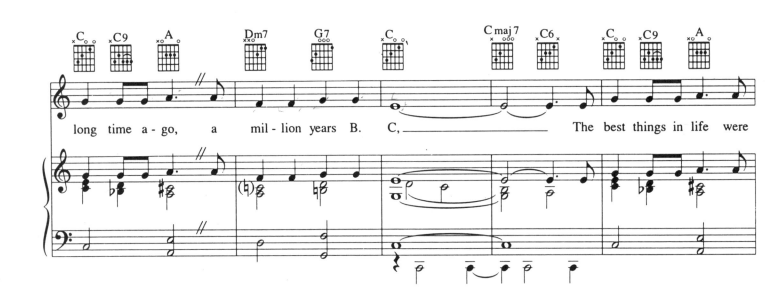

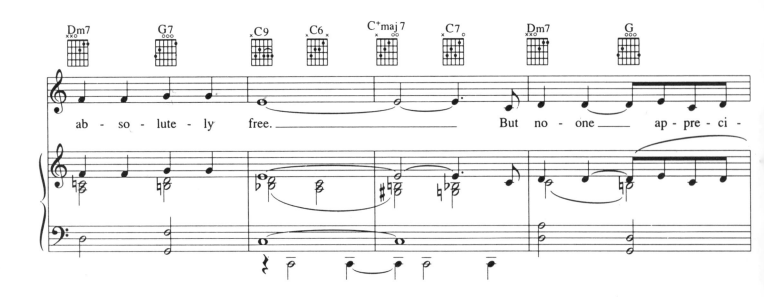

Chorus

For ev-'ry time it rains, it rains Pen-nies from hea - ven. ____

Don't you know each cloud con - tains Pen-nies from hea - ven? ____

You'll find your for-tune fall-ing all o-ver town. Be sure that

your um-brel-la is up-side-down. Trade them for a

In The Chapel In The Moonlight

Words & Music by Billy Hill.

The Way You Look Tonight

Music by Jerome Kern. Words by Dorothy Fields.

Swing Time, one of the finest of all Fred Astaire-Ginger Rogers pictures, featured Fred as a gambler/dancer, Ginger a dance instructress. At one point, Fred serenaded Ginger (who was off-screen in another room shampooing her hair). Music for the song was written by Jerome Kern and the lyrics were provided by Dorothy Fields. 'The Way You Look Tonight' deservedly won the Oscar for best song of its year.

Moderately

Some day when I'm aw-f'ly
love - ly, with your smile so

low, when the world is cold, I will feel a
warm, and your cheek so soft, there is noth-ing

glow just think - ing of you,
for me but to love you,

and the way you look to - night.
just the way you look to - night.

Oh, but you're With each

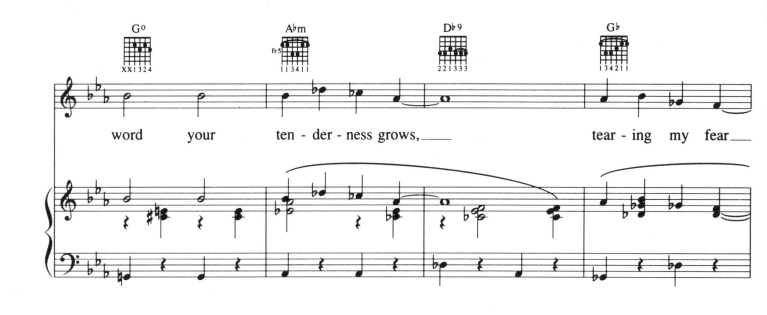

word your ten - der - ness grows, ____ tear - ing my fear ___

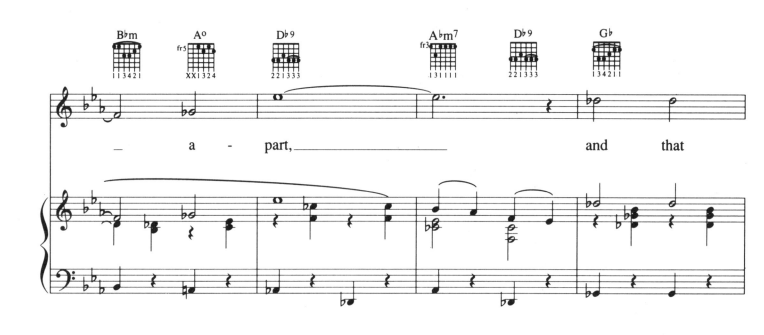

_ a - part, _____ and that

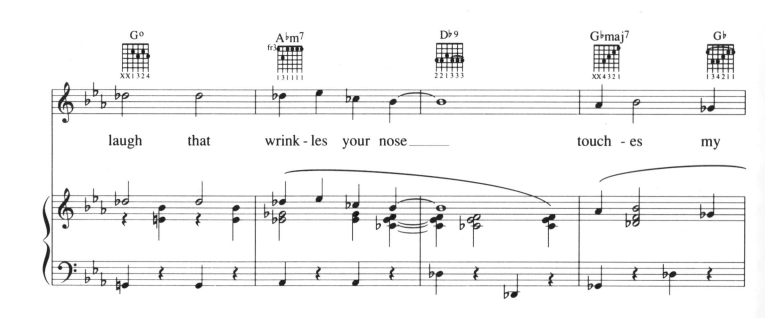

laugh that wrink - les your nose ____ touch - es my

fool - ish heart._____

Love - ly, nev - er, nev - er change,

keep that breath - less charm, won't you please ar - range it, 'cause I

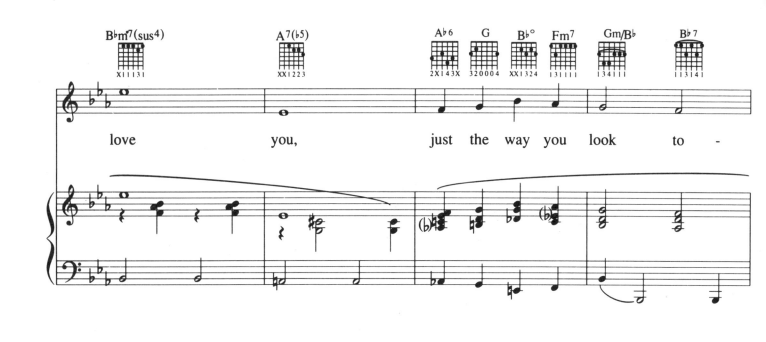

love you, just the way you look to-

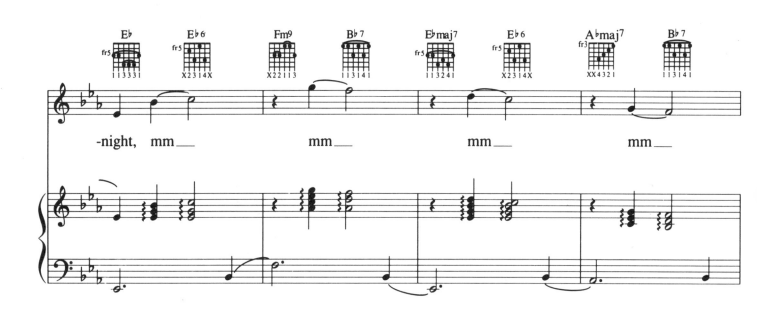

-night, mm___ mm___ mm___ mm___

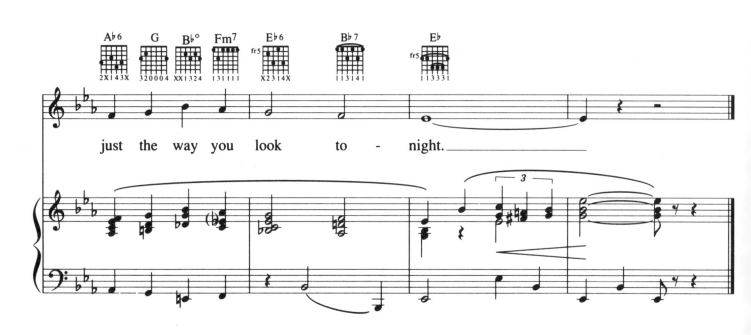

just the way you look to - night._____

An Apple For The Teacher

Words by Johnny Burke. Music by James V. Monaco.

Although the pleasant 1939 Bing Crosby film musical The Star Maker dealt with the life of composer Gus Edwards, the man who discovered Eleanor Powell and Eddie Cantor, it included only one of his own songs. The hit song was the newly composed 'An Apple For The Teacher' by two of Crosby's favourite writers, Johnny Burke and James V. Monaco.

226

All The Things You Are

Music by Jerome Kern. Words by Oscar Hammerstein II.

Very Warm For May opened on Broadway in November 1939, closing the following January. May was the heroine, chased by gangsters - hence it was very warm for her! The show contained one of the finest songs of that - or of any - year, 'All The Things You Are', which subsequently featured in the 1944 film Broadway Rhythm.

Moderately, with expression

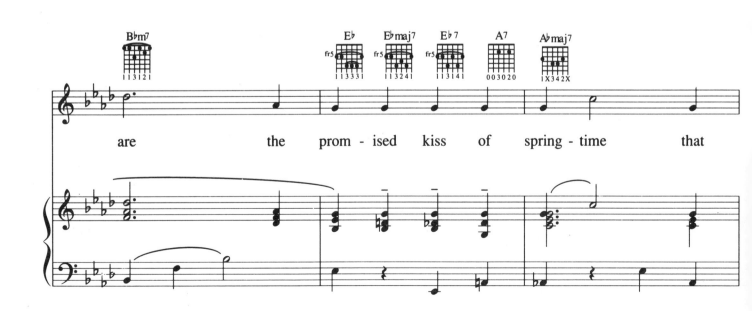

makes the lone - ly win - ter seem long. _____

_ You are the

breath - less hush of eve - ning that trem - bles on the

are. _____ Some

day my hap - py arms will hold you, and

some day I'll know that mo-ment di -

231

vine,   when all the things you are,   are

1. mine!

2. mine! _____

cresc.

sf   *molto rall.*

South Of The Border

Words & Music by Jimmy Kennedy & Michael Carr.

'South Of The Border (down Mexico Way)'
is a British song from 1939, written by the
well-known team of Michael Carr and
Jimmy Kennedy who were separately and
together responsible for some of the best
known novelties and romantic ballads of
the 30s and 40s. It was not only a British hit;
Bing Crosby also made a memorable hit
recording of the song.

Ross Parker and Hughie Charles' creative burst of activity in 1939 included one of the classic wartime hits 'We'll Meet Again' that was to become the theme song of the Force's Sweetheart, Vera Lynn, revived so memorably by Dame Vera herself during the televised VE Day commemorative celebrations in 1995.

We'll Meet Again

Words & Music by Ross Parker & Hughie Charles.

Moderately with expression

VERSE

Let's say good-bye with a smile dear,___ just for a while dear,___ we must
Af-ter the rain comes the rain-bow,___ you'll see the rain go,___ ne-ver

part,___ don't let the part-ing up-set you,___ I'll not for-
fear,___ we two can wait for to-mor-row,___ good-bye to

get you sweet-heart.
sor-row my dear.

CHORUS

We'll meet a-gain, don't know

237

Whispering Grass

Words by Fred Fisher.
Music by Doris Fisher.

Forever associated with The Inkspots who had a hit with the song in 1941, 'Whispering Grass' enjoyed a fresh lease of life in 1975 when two popular characters from the television comedy series It Ain't Half Hot Mum took it to No.1 for three weeks. They were 'Lofty', the diminutive Don Estelle, and the Sergeant-Major, played by Windsor Davies.

You pro-mised me, green grass, not to tell what you heard.

Whis-per-ing grass,_ say! you can't keep_ your word,__ keep your word._

CHORUS

Why do you whis - per, green grass? Why tell the trees what ain't

One of the most poignantly evocative of all songs about London, 'A Nightingale Sang In Berkeley Square' was introduced, in wartime, in the London musical revue New Faces by the elegant Judy Campbell. Sadly, she was not asked to record it. However, many others did - with great success, including Frank Sinatra and Tony Bennett.

A Nightingale Sang In Berkeley Square

Words by Eric Maschwitz. Music by Manning Sherwin.

All Or Nothing At All

Words & Music by Arthur Altman & Jack Lawrence.

If you blinked, you missed the modest musical Weekend Pass. It starred Martha O'Driscoll as a girl trying to join the Women's Army Corps in America. Its hit song has far outlived the picture. 'All Or Nothing At All', sung in the picture by the Delta Rhythm Boys, went on to become a classic standard, and was often sung by Frank Sinatra.

Moderately slow

fall. And if I fell under the spell of your call, I would be caught in the under-tow. So, you see I've got to say no! No! All or Noth-ing At All!

CODA All!

The Breeze And I

Words by Al Stillman.
Music by Ernesto Lecuona.

Cuban composer Ernesto Lecuona wrote many distinguished classical compositions. In 1940, United States music publishers took an interest in Latin American music and Lecuona was one of the beneficiaries. His piano composition 'Andalucia' formed the basis for the popular song 'The Breeze And I' with English words by Al Stillman.

249

The Last Time I Saw Paris

Music by Jerome Kern.
Words by Oscar Hammerstein II.

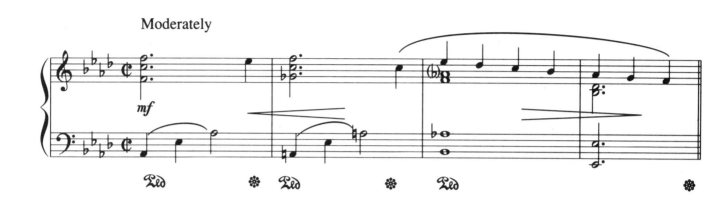

The last time I saw Par - is her heart was warm and

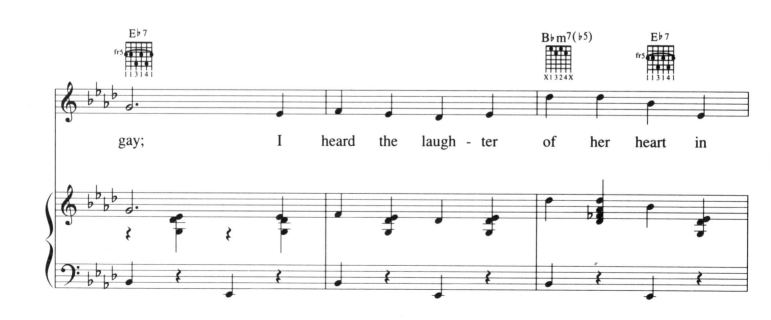

gay; I heard the laugh-ter of her heart in

ev' - ry street ca - fé. The last time I saw

Par - is, her trees were dressed for spring, and

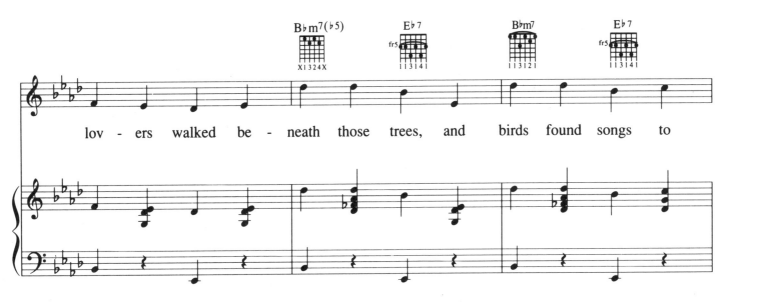

lov - ers walked be - neath those trees, and birds found songs to

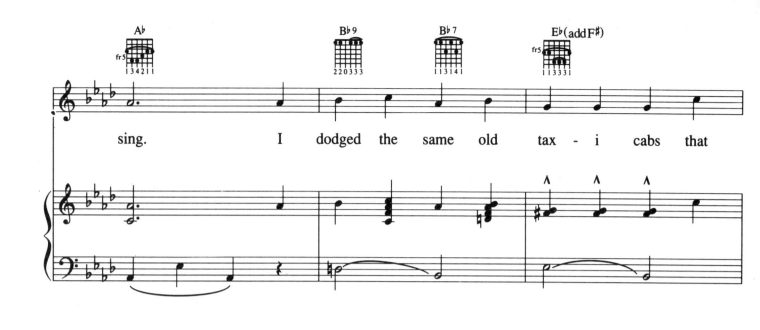

sing.   I   dodged   the   same   old   tax - i   cabs   that

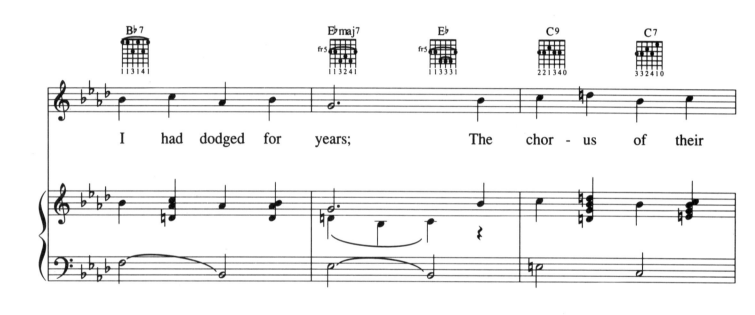

I   had   dodged   for   years;   The   chor - us   of   their

squeak - y   horns   was   mu - sic   to   my   ears.   The   last   time   I   saw

The Forties saw a sudden explosion of music from Latin America on to the popular music scene. 'Besame Mucho', a song from Mexico with music by Consuelo Velazquez, gained English lyrics by Sunny Skylar and became a hit in the 1944 film Follow The Boys and also in Club Havana. In 1995 Clarke Peters included the song in his Nat 'King' Cole show Unforgettable.

Besame Mucho

English Words by Sunny Skylar.
Music by Consuelo Velazquez.

Bé - sa - me, _____ Bé - sa - me mu - cho, _____
Bé - sa - me, _____ Bé - sa - me mu - cho, _____

each time I cling to your kiss I hear mu - sic di - vine, _____
co - mo si fue - ra es - ta no - che la úl - ti - ma vez, _____

Bé - - - - sa - me mu - cho, _____
Bé - - - - sa - me mu - cho, _____

Hold me my dar-ling and say that you'll al-ways be mine. _____
que ten-go mie-do per-der-te, per-der-te o-tra vez. _____

This joy is some-thing new, My arms en-fold-ing you, Nev-er knew this thrill be-
Quie-ro te-ner-te muy cer-ca, mi-rar-me en tus o-jos, ver-te jun-to a

fore, Who ev-er thought I'd be hold-ing you close to me,
mí, pien-sa que tal vez ma-ña-na yo ya es-ta-ré

Whisp-'ring "It's you I a-dore." Dear-est one, _____ If you should
le-jos, muy le-jos de ti. Bé-sa-me, _____ Bé-sa-me

There I've Said It Again

Words & Music by Redd Evans & Dave Mann.

Redd Evans and Dave Mann collaborated on a number of all-time standards, including 'No Moon At All,' and 'Don't Go To Strangers'. 'There I've Said It Again' was an immediate success, again in 1945 and subsequently in 1947 and 1964. Classic recordings feature Jimmy Young, Vaughn Monroe, Nat 'King' Cole and The Four Aces.

Billy Strayhorn, who was for so long Duke Ellington's pianist and arranger, composed Ellington's theme tune 'Take The 'A' Train'. It was featured in the film Reveille with Beverly in 1943, and used in the successful stage shows Bubbling Brown Sugar and Sophisticated Ladies. The 'A' Train is one of New York's subway trains that passes through Harlem.

Take The 'A' Train

Words & Music by Billy Strayhorn

I'll Remember April

Words & Music by Don Raye, Gene de Paul & Patricia Johnson.

Bud Abbott and Lou Costello played hot dog sellers on a dude ranch in the comedy film musical Ride 'Em Cowboy. Don Raye and Gene de Paul contributed some memorable songs, and Ella Fitzgerald was around to sing them. 'I'll Remember April' was the big hit – and even inspired a further film bearing the song's title.

This love-ly day will leng-then in to ev-'ning, we'll sigh good-bye to all we've ev-er had. A - lone, where we have walked to-geth-er, I'll Re-mem-ber A-pril and be glad.

Long Ago And Far Away

Music by Jerome Kern.
Words by Ira Gershwin.

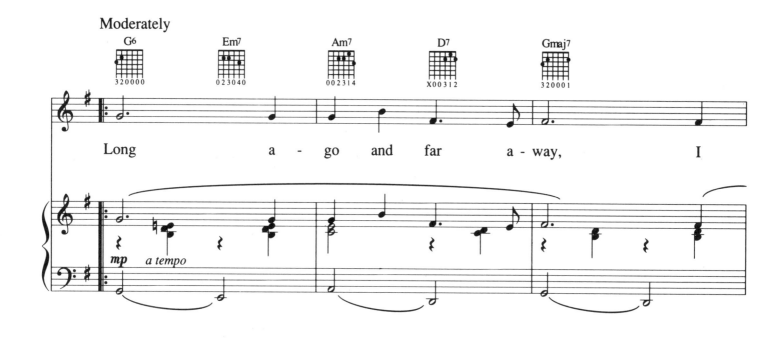

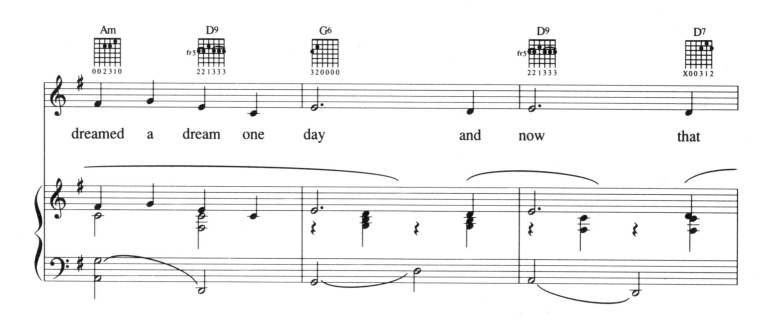

dream is here be - side me. Long the

skies were ov - er - cast, but now the clouds have

passed: you're here at last!

Here's a song partly written by three of the greatest names in 40's swing - bandleaders Harry James, Duke Ellington and saxophone genius Johnny Hodges with Don George - the latter's credits also include 'The Yellow Rose Of Texas'. The song was featured in the film The Man From Oklahoma.

I'm Beginning To See The Light

Words & Music by Harry James, Duke Ellington, Johnny Hodges & Don George.

I nev-er cared much for moon-lit skies,___ I nev-er wink back at fire - flies,___ But now that the stars are in your eyes,___ I'm Be - gin-ning To See The Light.___ I nev-er went in for af-ter glow, Or can-dle-light on the mis-tle-toe,___ But

Take Me To Your Heart Again
(La Vie En Rose)

Music by R. S. Louiguy.
English Lyric by Frank Eyton.

Steady 2 beat

Verse

How soon the shad-ows would de-part, If you would give me back your heart, How life would take a ro-sy hue; Could we be-gin it all a-new. You're mine what-

ev - er may be - fall,_____ Life is short, and love is

all._____ Take me to your heart a - gain, Let's

make a start a - gain, For - giv - ing and for - get -

-ting; Take me to your heart a - gain, And

say - ing "I love you," Then we'll nev - er part a - gain, If

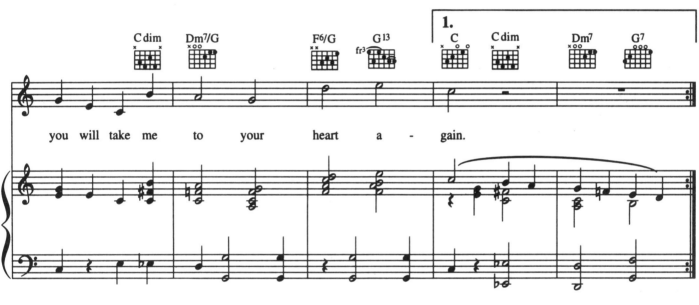

you will take me to your heart a - gain.

1.

2.

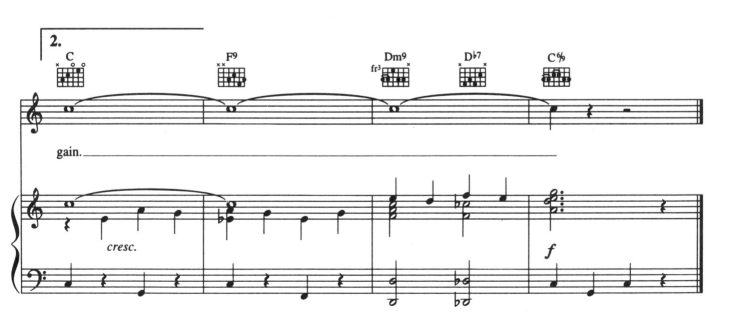

gain.

cresc.

f

Cruising Down The River

Words & Music by Eily Beadell & Nell Tollerton.

The winning entry in a 1945 songwriting contest, 'Cruising Down The River' was the work of two English writers who were never again to enjoy such success. The song proved so popular abroad that in 1953 Columbia Pictures starred Dick Haymes in a musical about a singer who inherits a riverboat. Its title? Cruising Down The River.

Ballerina

Music by Carl Sigman.
Words by Bob Russell.

Vaughn Monroe and Bing Crosby both had hits with Carl Sigman and Bob Russell's 'Ballerina', a 1947 ballad by two experienced writers who individually would continue to create hits for decades to come - Sigman with 'Ebb Tide', 'Answer Me' and 'What Now My Love?' and Bob Russell with 'Little Green Apples' and 'He Ain't Heavy...He's My Brother'.

1. Dance Bal - le - ri - na dance and do your pir - ou - ette in rhy - thm with your ach - ing heart.
Dance bal - le - ri - na dance you must - n't once for -

2. Whirl Bal - le - ri - na whirl and just ig - nore the chair that's emp - ty in the sec - ond row.
This is your mo - ment girl al - though he's not out

1946, lyricist Frank Loesser was also writing
own music. For Neptune's Daughter,
came up with a cute novelty number for
imming star Esther Williams and
cardo Montalban as her South American
mantic interest. The song deservedly
on the Academy Award for best film
ng for 1948.

Baby It's Cold Outside

Words & Music by Frank Loesser.

Loesserando

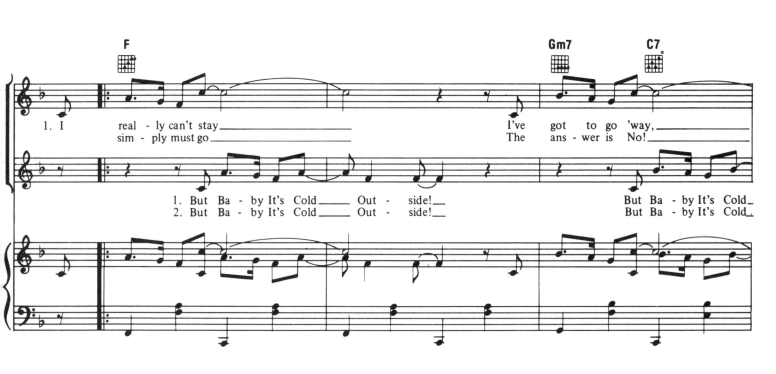

1. I real - ly can't stay___ I've got to go 'way,___
   sim - ply must go___ The ans - wer is No!___

1. But Ba - by It's Cold___ Out - side!___ But Ba - by It's Cold_
2. But Ba - by It's Cold___ Out - side!___ But Ba - by It's Cold_

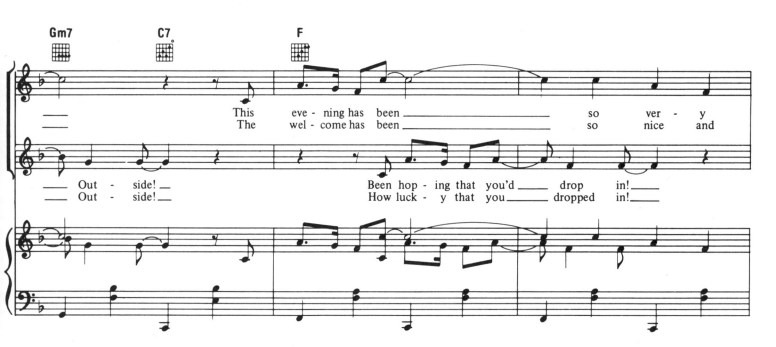

This eve - ning has been ___ so ver - y
The wel - come has been ___ so nice and

___ Out - side! ___ Been hop - ing that you'd ___ drop in! ___
___ Out - side! ___ How luck - y that you ___ dropped in! ___

neigh-bors might think ____ Say, What's in this drink? ____
got to get home ____ Say, lend me a comb ____

But, ba-by,it's bad ____ out there ____ No cabs to be had ____
But, ba-by,you'd freeze ____ out there ____ It's up to your knees ____

I wish I knew how ____ to break the
You've real-ly been grand ____ but don't you break

____ out there ____ Your eyes are like star-light now ____
____ out there ____ I thrill when you touch ____ my hand ____

spell ____ I ought to say "No, no,
see ____ There's bound to be talk to-

I'll take your hat ____ your hair looks swell
How can you do ____ this thing to me

284

Johnny Mercer provided the English lyrics for one of the great romantic ballads from France - 'Les Feuilles Mortes'. Jacques Prevert, author of the original words, was one of France's greatest poets of the 30s and 40s. Joseph Kosma wrote countless film scores and popular songs - but none as popular as 'Autumn Leaves'.

Autumn Leaves
(Les Feuilles Mortes)

Music by Joseph Kosma. Words by Jacques Prevert.
English Lyrics by Johnny Mercer

The fall-ing leaves _____ drift by my win-dow, _____ the au-tumn leaves _____ of red and gold. I see your lips, _____ the sum-mer kiss - es, _____ the sun-burned hands _____ I used to hold. Since you

went a - way ___ the days grow long, _____ and soon I'll hear _____ old win - ter's

song. But I miss you most of all my dar - ling, when

au - tumn leaves start to fall. C'est une chan - son, _____ qui nous res -

sem - ble, ___ toi tu m'ai - mois _____ et je t'ai - mais. Nous vi - vions